SPINOSAURUS

and Other Dinosaurs of Africa

by Dougal Dixon

illustrated by
Steve Weston and James Field

PICTURE WINDOW BOOKS
Minneapolis, Minnesota

Picture Window Books
5115 Excelsior Boulevard
Suite 232
Minneapolis, MN 55416
877-845-8392
www.picturewindowbooks.com

Printed in the United States of America.

Library of Congress Cataloging-in-Publication Data
Dixon, Dougal.
Spinosaurus and other dinosaurs of Africa / by
Dougal Dixon ; illustrated by Steve Weston &
James Field.
p. cm. — (Dinosaur find)
Includes bibliographical references and index.
ISBN-13: 978-1-4048-2260-3 (library binding)
ISBN-10: 1-4048-2260-7 (library binding)
ISBN-13: 978-1-4048-2266-5 (paperback)
ISBN-10: 1-4048-2266-6 (paperback)
1. Dinosaurs–Africa–Juvenile literature. I. Weston, Steve,
ill. II. Field, James, 1959- ill. III. Title.
QE861.5.D649 2007
567.9096–dc22   2006028004

Acknowledgments
This book was produced for Picture Window Books by
Bender Richardson White, U.K.

Illustrations by James Field (cover and pages 4–5, 9,
13, 17, 19) and Steve Weston (pages 7, 11, 15, 21).
Diagrams by Stefan Chabluk.

Photographs: Digital Vision pages 8, 12. istockphotos
pages 6 (Enfys), 10 (Yuval Sive), 14 (Simone van den
Berg), 16 (Ralph Paprzycki), 18 (Vladimir Pomortsev),
20 (Nick Berrisford).

Consultant: John Stidworthy, Scientific Fellow of
the Zoological Society, London, and former
Lecturer in the Education Department, Natural History
Museum, London.

Reading Adviser: Susan Kesselring, M.A., Literacy
Educator, Rosemount–Apple Valley–Eagan
(Minnesota) School District

Types of dinosaurs

In this book, a red shape at the top of a left-hand page shows the animal was a meat-eater. A green shape shows it was a plant-eater.

Just how big—or small—were they?

Dinosaurs were many different sizes. We have compared their size to one of the following:

Chicken
2 feet (60 centimeters) tall
Weight 6 pounds (2.7 kilograms)

Adult person
6 feet (1.8 meters) tall
Weight 170 pounds (76.5 kg)

Elephant
10 feet (3 m) tall
Weight 12,000 pounds
(5,400 kg)

TABLE OF CONTENTS

Life in Africa. 4

Brachytrachelopan. 6

Rugops 8

Paralititan 10

Kentrosaurus 12

Nqwebasaurus 14

Ouranosaurus 16

Spinosaurus. 18

Heterodontosaurus 20

Where Did They Go?. . . 22

Glossary. 23

Find Out More 24

Index 24

WHAT'S INSIDE?

Dinosaurs! These dinosaurs lived in places that now form Africa. Find out how they survived millions of years ago and what they have in common with today's animals.

LIFE IN AFRICA

Dinosaurs lived between 230 million and 65 million years ago. The world did not look the same then. Much of the land and many of the seas were not in the same places as they are now. Today, Africa is famous for its animal life. In dinosaur times, many animals lived in the region, but they were quite different.

A distant herd of *Ouranosaurus* were stalked by two ferocious *Spinosaurus*. These dinosaurs, in turn, were hunted by the fierce *Rugops*. Life as a dinosaur could be very dangerous in the land that is now Africa!

BRACHYTRACHELOPAN

Brachytrachelopan was an odd creature. It was a close relative of long-necked, plant-eating dinosaurs, but it had a short neck. Instead of eating from the tops of tall trees like its relatives, this dinosaur grazed on small plants.

Grazing today

Modern horses graze on grass. They bow their heads low to eat, much like *Brachytrachelopan* did long ago.

Size Comparison

6

A family of *Brachytrachelopan* fed together in open ground. They ate the low-growing ferns and plants called horsetails.

RUGOPS

Pronunciation:
ROO-gops

Rugops was built to be a meat-eater. Forceful hind legs helped it chase down prey. Then it used strong hands and long claws to grab and tear into the animals it hunted. Powerful jaws and sharp teeth also helped *Rugops* at feeding time.

Fierce teeth today

Modern bears use their teeth and claws to kill animals and to tear flesh from bones, much like *Rugops* did millions of years ago.

Size Comparison

8

With powerful legs, a large body, and pointed teeth, *Rugops* was a frightening sight. Its growls and grunts probably made it even more fearsome.

PARALITITAN

Pronunciation:
PAR-uh-LEE-tye-TAN

What a monster! *Paralititan* is believed to have been the biggest of the African dinosaurs. *Paralititan* lived near the coasts. It probably crossed the wide mouths of rivers to reach feeding grounds on the opposite banks.

Big swimmers today

Despite their size, modern elephants can wade and swim across rivers when looking for food, much like *Paralititan* once did.

Size Comparison

Paralititan was big and strong. It could wade shoulder-deep through water, where few other dinosaurs would follow.

KENTROSAURUS

Pronunciation:
KEN-tro-SAW-rus

Kentrosaurus was an armored dinosaur. It had two rows of pointed plates running the length of its neck and back. *Kentrosaurus* also had spikes sticking out of its shoulders and tail. It used this armor to fend off enemies.

Big, fast runners today

Wildebeests are big plant-eaters that can move very quickly to escape danger, just as *Kentrosaurus* did.

Size Comparison

Although weighed down by its armor, *Kentrosaurus* could move quickly to escape a forest fire. Other speedy dinosaurs would join the run to safety.

13

NQWEBASAURUS

Pronunciation:
Nn-KWE-ba-SAW-rus

Not all the dinosaurs of the area were big brutes. *Nqwebasaurus* was only the size of a chicken. But this dinosaur could run swiftly on its hind legs. It hunted insects and other small animals through the undergrowth.

Long fingers today

The modern sifaka uses its long fingers and claws to gather food and grasp branches, much like *Nqwebasaurus* did.

Size Comparison

Nqwebasaurus had long fingers and claws on its hands. It could poke them into holes in tree trunks and wiggle out grubs and other small creatures that burrowed there.

OURANOSAURUS

Pronunciation:
oo-RAN-uh-SAW-rus

Big, plant-eating *Ouranosaurus* had tall spines along its back. These may have supported a brightly colored sail. The sail might have been used for signaling other dinosaurs or to help warm or cool the dinosaur's body.

Desert living today

The modern camel has a hump to store food and can go for days without water. It is built for desert living, as *Ouranosaurus* was.

Size Comparison

Ouranosaurus may have used its sail like a fan to cool down. It also may have used the sail to trap sunlight and warm its body.

SPINOSAURUS

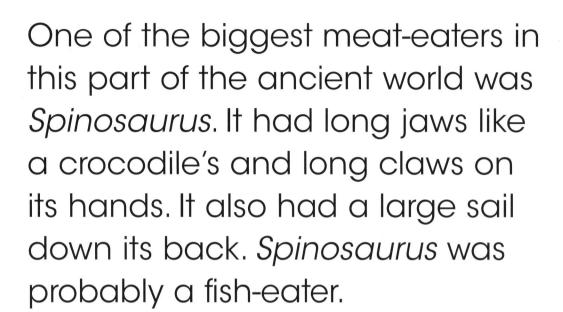

Pronunciation:
SPY-nuh-SAW-rus

One of the biggest meat-eaters in this part of the ancient world was *Spinosaurus*. It had long jaws like a crocodile's and long claws on its hands. It also had a large sail down its back. *Spinosaurus* was probably a fish-eater.

Gripping jaws today

The modern gharial is a fish-eating crocodile. It has long, thin jaws and jagged teeth, like *Spinosaurus* once did.

Size Comparison

Spinosaurus used its sharp, pointed teeth to hold on to slippery prey.

19

HETERODONTOSAURUS

Pronunciation:
HET-ur-oh-DON-toe-SAW-rus

Heterodontosaurus was a small dinosaur. It was about the size of a badger. This dinosaur lived in the sandy areas of what is now Africa. With teeth of different shapes and sizes, *Heterodontosaurus* could pluck and chew desert plants.

Desert-living today

Some modern lizards live in hot deserts and feed on the desert plants like *Heterodontosaurus* did.

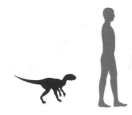

Size Comparison

Life was harsh in the ancient deserts. *Heterodontosaurus* tried to stay out of the sun much of the time and had to hide from sandstorms.

21

WHERE DID THEY GO?

Dinosaurs are extinct, which means that none of them are alive today. Scientists study rocks and fossils to find clues about what happened to dinosaurs.

People have different explanations about the extinction. Some people think a huge asteroid that hit Earth caused all sorts of climate changes. This then caused the dinosaurs to die. Others think volcanic eruptions caused the climate to change and that killed the dinosaurs. No one knows for sure, though.

GLOSSARY

armor—protective covering of plates, horns, spikes, or clubs used for fighting

brutes—strong and dangerous animals

claws—tough, usually curved fingernails or toenails

ferns—plants with finely divided leaves known as fronds; ferns are common in damp woods and along rivers

horsetails—simple, non-branching plants related to ferns, with jointed stems and tiny leaves

plate—a large, flat, usually tough structure on the body

prey—animals that are hunted by other animals for food; the hunters are known as predators

sail—a thin, upright structure on the back of some animals

signal—to make a sign, warning, or hint

spines—sharp, pointed growths

To Learn More

At the Library

Clark, Neil, and William Lindsay. *1001 Facts About Dinosaurs.* New York: Backpack Books, Dorling Kindersley, 2002.

Dixon, Dougal. *Dougal Dixon's Amazing Dinosaurs.* Honesdale, Pa.: Boyds Mills Press, 2000.

Holtz, Thomas, and Michael Brett-Surman. *Dinosaur Field Guide.* New York: Random House, 2001.

On the Web

FactHound offers a safe, fun way to find Web sites related to this book. All of the sites on FactHound have been researched by our staff.

1. Visit *www.facthound.com*
2. Type in this special code: 1404822607
3. Click on the FETCH IT button.

Your trusty FactHound will fetch the best Web sites for you!

Index

armor, 12, 13
Brachytrachelopan, 6–7
claws, 8, 14, 15, 18
hands, 8, 15, 18
Heterodontosaurus, 20–21
insects, 14
jaws, 8, 9, 18

Kentrosaurus, 12–13
legs, 8, 9, 14
neck, 6, 12
Nqwebasaurus, 14–15
Ouranosaurus, 4, 16–17
Paralititan, 10–11
plates, 12

Rugops, 4, 8–9
sails, 16, 17, 18
spikes, 12
Spinosaurus, 4, 18–19
tail, 12
teeth, 8, 9, 18, 19, 20
trees, 6, 15

Look for all of the books in the Dinosaur Find series:

Agustinia and Other Dinosaurs of Central and South America
Aletopelta and Other Dinosaurs of the West Coast
Allosaurus and Other Dinosaurs of the Rockies
Ankylosaurus and Other Mountain Dinosaurs
Centrosaurus and Other Dinosaurs of Cold Places
Ceratosaurus and Other Fierce Dinosaurs
Coelophysis and Other Dinosaurs of the South
Deltadromeus and Other Shoreline Dinosaurs
Dromaeosaurus and Other Dinosaurs of the North
Giganotosaurus and Other Big Dinosaurs
Maiasaura and Other Dinosaurs of the Midwest
Minmi and Other Dinosaurs of Australia

Neovenator and Other Dinosaurs of Europe
Nodosaurus and Other Dinosaurs of the East Coast
Ornithomimus and Other Fast Dinosaurs
Plateosaurus and Other Desert Dinosaurs
Saltopus and Other First Dinosaurs
Scutellosaurus and Other Small Dinosaurs
Spinosaurus and Other Dinosaurs of Africa
Stegosaurus and Other Plains Dinosaurs
Styracosaurus and Other Last Dinosaurs
Therizinosaurus and Other Dinosaurs of Asia
Triceratops and Other Forest Dinosaurs
Tyrannosaurus and Other Dinosaurs of North America